H.O.P.E.

Brittany Monk

Cadmus Publishing
www.cadmuspublishing.com

Copyright © 2022 Brittany Monk

Cover art by Tad M. Bomboli

Published by Cadmus Publishing
www.cadmuspublishing.com
Port Angeles, WA

ISBN: 978-1-63751-294-4

All rights reserved. Copyright under Berne Copyright Convention, Universal Copyright Convention, and Pan-American Copyright Convention. No part of this book may be reproduced, stored in a retrieval system, or transmitted in any form, or by any means, electronic, mechanical, photocopying, recording or otherwise, without prior permission of the author.

The author would love to hear from you! Please reach out to Brittany at BrittanyMonk23@outlook.com. You can also find more about her and her books at www.cadmuspublishing.com/authors/BrittanyMonk

Table of Contents

Follow the Stars 1
Encourage Yourself 4
Know Your Worth 7
Let Go and Hold On 10
Gratitude Brings Good 13
Prepare to Receive 16
Plant the Seed 19
Free Your Mind 22
Believe in Magic 25
Positive Perspective 28
Dare to Dream 31
Unveil the Unseen 34
Faith, No Fear 37
Breathe 40
Be a Lighthouse 43
Spread the Jewels 47
The Closing: Uncovering the Meaning of H.O.P.E. 51
H.O.P.E. Challenges 55
- Follow the Stars Challenge 56
- Encourage Yourself Challenge 58
- Know Your Worth Challenge 60
- Let Go and Hold On Challenge 62
- Gratitude Brings Good Challenge 64
- Prepare to Receive Challenge 66
- Plant the Seed Challenge 68
- Free Your Mind Challenge 70
- Believe in Magic Challenge 72
- Positive Perspective Challenge 74

- Dare to Dream Challenge. 76
- Unveil the Unseen Challenge 78
- Faith, No Fear Challenge .80
- Breathe Challenge. 82
- Be a Lighthouse Challenge 84
- Spread the Jewels Challenge 86

"Before you speak, ask yourself: is it kind, is it necessary, is it true, does it improve the silence?"

- Shirdi Sai Baba

Foreword

What is your story? If a stranger asked you this question today, what would you say? How would you tell your story? The answer to these questions have been unclear to me until recently. I know what I've experienced in the past. I know the pain I've felt and the pain I've caused. I know the mistakes that I've made and the consequence that have followed.

My past consisted of various moments of darkness. I experienced many forms of abuse throughout my childhood and adolescence - sexual, physical, and emotional. I've experienced mental disruptions like depression, anxiety, and PTSD. I've witnessed those same mental disruptions take over the lives of loved ones and addiction take its course in their lives as well.

I fled from one bad situation to another searching for security. I struggled with codependency and acceptance of abuse. My self-worth was damaged severely and I felt hopeless. Eventually, I made a detrimental mistake that led me to receive a 35 year prison sentence at just 17 years old. At that point, I felt that I had nothing left. Still I didn't want that to be my ending.

I didn't want my story to be one of failure and defeat, but one of the hope that allowed me to move forward.

There may be parts of my past that you can relate to. Maybe there are parts that you too have experienced or witnessed. There may have been moments in your life when you believed it was the end of the road and you had nothing left to give. You may not have realized it yet, but in that very moment you had everything to give and everything to receive.

If you are living in that moment today, let that knowledge give you a glimmer of hope. Let that hope be the ink in which you rewrite your own story. Your mistakes do not make your story. Your pain does not make your story. YOU are what makes your story, and you have say so in how your story is told.

The darkness that existed in my past was mine. It may have been different from yours. However, it was in that darkness that I discovered the brilliance of my own light. I discovered my hope, my faith, and my power to love. I discovered the methods that helped me to heal, to grow, and to shine.

Throughout the pages of this book, I will share those methods with you. I will share with you all that I have learned. And my hope is that the pages of this book inspire you, encourage you, and empower you. That this book motivates you to believe that no matter how dark your life may seem, there is a light within you that the darkness cannot subdue.

My hope is that after you read this book, you understand that you are worthy of the best that life has to offer. That you are magnificent and powerful. That you have the power to make your story beautiful and bright. I hope that you use these methods to H.O.P.E. and take it a step further by discovering your own methods. You have the power to not only make a difference in the world, but to be the difference.

Follow the Stars

"Two men looked out from prison bars, one saw the mud, the other saw stars."

- Dale Carnegie

Before the invention of the compass and the clock, humans used the sky to determine time and direction. We followed the stars and they led us to our destination each and every time. If ever we got lost along the way, it was because of our own misunderstanding. The compass and the clock may glitch and misdirect us, but the stars are never guilty of misguidance.

When I was a young girl, my mother used tacky glue to stick glow-in-the-dark stars to the ceiling of my bedroom. There had to be about a hundred of them. I had trouble sleeping most nights lost in my thoughts. I would count the stars to quiet my mind, and the stars guided me to sleep.

> *The compass and the clock may glitch and misdirect us, but the stars are never guilty of misguidance.*

Throughout my life, I have depended on the stars to guide me. Anytime the image of a star came into my view, I received that as reassurance that I was heading in the right direction. When anxiety and fear threatened to take over, I would picture myself counting the stars in my childhood bedroom. Those stars still give me a sense of peace and hope.

In your life, you will find the thing that will resonate with you and be your symbol of hope. It may not be a star, that is only my example. Maybe for you it is a number, or a butterfly, or a specific color. Maybe it is a word that you hear. Whatever it is, when you find it, let it guide you. It is a sign that you are on the right frequency.

No matter who you are, what background you come from, or what mistakes you have made, you can turn your life into something beautiful. If you are headed down the wrong path, you can choose a new path. You can decide today that you will take a new direction, make a better decision. You are not obligated to your past. Your mistakes do not make you. You are not the same person today as you were yesterday, and you will not be the same person tomorrow.

You are constantly evolving into a new version of yourself - let each version be a better one. If you get discouraged you can ask the Universe for reassurance and guidance. You will receive it. Be guided by your symbol of hope. Today is a new opportunity to start over. Today you can choose the direction of love, the direction of happiness, the direction of perfect health, the direction of peace. You can choose to follow the stars and let them lead you to finding your profound purpose in this life. Let the stars lead you to your joy. Be empowered to take a step forth in a better direction.

Encourage Yourself

"Make the most of yourself by fanning the tiny, inner sparks of possibility into flames of achievement."

- Golda Meir

Sometimes you have to be your own motivator, your own support system, and your own accountability partner. Sometimes you have to be your own biggest fan. When no one else believes in you, believe in yourself. When no one else inspires you, inspire yourself. When no one else pushes you, push yourself. Sometimes you have to be the one to encourage yourself.

Let your reflection be your prompt and speak words of encouragement over your circumstances. If you are feeling defeated, speak victory over yourself. If you are feeling sad, speak happiness over yourself. If you are feeling sickness, speak health over yourself. Whatever negativity you are feeling or thinking, counter those feelings and thoughts with positive affirmations. Remember all of your achievements and moments of happiness and let those moments encourage you.

Often times you look to others to encourage you. You see the success of others and you believe that your own success is possible. You see the victory of others and you believe in your own victory. You see the healing of others and you believe in your own healing. You see the freedom of others and you believe in your own freedom, as you should.

However, there isn't always someone around to look to for empowerment. There isn't always someone around that's embodying the vision you have for yourself. Maybe no one is there to uplift you, to make you smile, to tell you "You can do it." Maybe there isn't any good news around you and you're feeling that you're on the wrong frequency.

This is your moment. Here is your good news: You CAN do it. You ARE great. You WILL be victorious. When no one is there to tell you, tell yourself. You are responsible for your own happiness, your own smile, and your own greatness. Be your own muse - your life is your masterpiece. Make it colorful and add a little glitter when necessary.

It's helpful when there are outside influences to give us an extra push when we need it. But everything you need to succeed comes from within you. You hold the match to ignite your own fuse. You have the oxygen necessary to will the fire to grow. You are the torch that holds that flame.

It is your purpose to find what brings you joy in this life and reach your full potential. Motivate yourself to reach new heights. Be supportive of your own dreams and aspirations.

Create your masterpiece and hold yourself accountable in making it beautiful. Cheer yourself on from the sidelines and believe that you can do it. Remember that even the word *impossible* says, "I'm possible." You CAN do anything. If this is what you tell yourself, then you WILL succeed.

> *Create your masterpiece and hold yourself accountable in making it beautiful.*

Know Your Worth

"There is no passion to be found playing small - in settling for a life that is less than the one you are capable of living."

- Nelson Mandela

How many times have you settled for less than you're worth? Well, I'm here to tell you - those days are OVER. You are worth all of the good that life has to offer. You are not defined by the opinions of others. You are worth all of the good that life has to offer. You are not defined by you past. You are not defined by the opinions of others. You are defined by what you believe about yourself.

Some say that the past is the best predication of the future. That is not truth. The fact is, what you learn from the past will impact how you respond in the future. Growth is essential in this case.

> *You are defined by what you believe about yourself.*

You have made mistakes in the past. Maybe you have fallen a time or two. But you're still standing. And the fact that you are reading this today, that you are searching for answers on how to keep your hope alive, speaks volumes of your determination to get up and try again.

Failure does not exist unless you fail to try again. You are worth a second chance. You are worth abundance. You are worth love. Even if you fumble the ball, you will recover it as long as you believe in yourself.

Guilt can also play a role in what we feel we deserve in life. When you've hurt someone and you harbor guilt for your actions, it can hinder you from moving forward. Remember that the path of growth starts with admittance and forgiveness. Forgiveness starts with you.

It is important that you forgive yourself for the mistakes you have made. By hurting others you have also hurt yourself. Take the time you need to reflect on the decisions you've made; however, be mindful that you have to sustain forward movement. Do not become stagnant and allow yourself to get stuck in a rut of self-pity and gloom. Pick yourself up, dust yourself off, and take one step forward at a time.

We go through many experiences that can impact the way we perceive ourselves. The opinions of others can also chip away at your self-esteem if you allow it. But there is no validation of your worth in the things others believe about you. Your worth is what YOU believe it to be. You are important. You are valuable. Most importantly, you are worth it.

Let Go and Hold On

―⸺∘⸺∘⸺―

"Step out of the history that is holding you back. Step into the story you are willing to create."

- Oprah Winfrey

There are things in life we have to let go of in order to hold on to things that are most valuable to us. Letting go is an action that has to be done with all of your being. Whether it is a material, a person, a habit, a circumstance, or condition that you are holding on to, you have to let go of it with your mind, body, and soul.

The ability to let go comes with knowing your worth and knowing what things, people, and circumstances are worth holding on to. That ability also comes with growth. People are like plants in this way.

There are many different types of plants that grow at different speeds and in different directions. This can also depend on the soil, fertilizer, and care the plant is given.

For example, rosebuds typically bloom within about 14 days and bloom repeatedly in cycles of 6 to 8 weeks. In comparison, a cactus may take 2 to 3 years to grow just a few centimeters. Does the rosebud wait on the cactus to catch up before it blooms? No.

Like plants, people grow at different speeds and in different directions. If you are moving forward at a swifter pace than another person, do you stop your growth and wait on them to catch up? Do you stay in a relationship because you refuse to let go although you have been unhappy for years? Do you refuse to let go of the grudges you hold? If you are refusing to let go of those things that are weighing you down, how will you grab on to the hand that might very well pull you up?

Ask yourself: Why am I refusing to let go? What might I gain from making room in my life for better things? Most of the time, we don't want to let go because we fear that we have lost time by putting our efforts into something or someone for so long. You don't want to miss out on what could have been. All you are doing is further exerting your energy on what you don't want.

Take charge of your life. Fertilize and nourish your soil. Practice healthy self-care. Release the tension of negativity and your dependency on external happenings from your life. Hold on to the happiness that lives within you.

You are responsible for your own happiness. As you evolve, so does your perception of the world around you. Focus on what you want to have in your life: people, things, and circumstances. If something is weighing you down as you travel through life, lighten your load. Only hold on to what brings you joy.

Letting go is an act of faith. It is the faith and belief that if you let go of this bad thing, something better will come into your life. It is believing that if you set higher standards for yourself, your life will begin to improve in order to meet those standards. It is the belief that healing is happening in your life and you deserve it. Because you do deserve it.

> *It is believing that if you set higher standards for yourself, your life will begin to improve in order to meet those standards.*

Let go of the prickly cacti and hold on to the beautiful rose. Hold on to happiness. Hold on to forgiveness and understanding. Hold on to better opportunities. Hold on to the good in your life. Hold on to things that are most valuable to you. Let go of the bad and hold on to the good. You might be amazed by the results.

GRATITUDE BRINGS GOOD

"As we express our gratitude, we must never forget that the highest appreciation is not to utter words, but to live by them."

- John F. Kennedy

Feeling good about your life and the good coming into your life now is essential to receiving more good. Feeling happiness, joy, excitement, harmoniousness, and prosperousness wills the power of the Universe to move people, things, and circumstances in your life favorably. However, to bring good into your life at maximum efficiency, you must feel gratitude.

Gratitude is the state of thankfulness for all of the things in your life. If you are not feeling and showing gratitude for your life, then you are taking for granted what you have. Taking anything for granted blocks the good that you wish to receive. It also ensures that what you do have, you will lose.

You may say the words "thank you" many times a day, but what are you feeling? Are you feeling that you're grateful for what you have, but it still isn't enough? Thoughts and feelings of not enough will produce results of not enough. If you want abundance, you must feel abundance and truly be thankful for the abundance in your life.

Life is full of wonders that are worthy of your attention and appreciation. The beauty of nature - the magnificence of the oceans that inhabit all of the beautiful forms of marine life, the trees that dance in the wind and provide you with an unlimited supply of oxygen, the crystal blue sky and its changing colors as the sun sets and rises for you. Your health - the fact that you are able to breathe, walk, and run the ability to use your senses, smell sweet fragrances, hear music and the laughter of children, see the eagle soar through the sky, taste the first sip of coffee in the morning, and feel the grass beneath your bare feet.

> *When you focus your thoughts on what you have to be thankful for, you are made aware of the good you have preciously overlooked.*

If ever you are feeling that your blessings have run out, take a moment to consider the things you may very well be taking for granted. When you focus your thoughts on what you have to be thankful for, you are made aware of the good you have preciously overlooked. Be thankful that you have lived to see such wonders, and feel gratitude for the endless blessings that are entering into your life as you read these words.

Your gratitude should reach beyond your own life. When others around you receive good news of blessings raining into their lives, you should be excited about their good news as well. If the good news of others is presented to you, then that is confirmation that you are putting positive energy into the Universe and you are on a good news frequency. Feel gratitude for the blessings and opportunities of others. Give gratitude to others. Feel joy for the good in their lives as well as the good in yours.

Gratitude is the glue that wills good to stick to you and stay in your life. If you are thankful for what you want as if you have it now, then gratitude will bring good into your life. However, once you receive the good that you have requested, you must continuously feel gratitude for having it, so that it will adhere to you. Let gratitude be your tool to manifest all of the blessings that your life can contain.

Prepare to Receive

"The more you see yourself as what you'd like to become, and act as if what you want is already there, the more you'll activate those dormant forces that will collaborate to transform your dream into reality."

- Wayne Dyer

Now that you have made room in your life for better people, things, and circumstances, preparation is the next step for you to take in order to bring into fruition the best version of your life.

In order to receive anything, good or bad, you have to believe that it is coming. Remember that to believe is to feel that something is truth.

Once you have decided upon what you want in your life, put in the request. Be very specific in the details of your desires. Know that once you have made your request, your belief that you will receive it is what will bring it into your life. Feel that the receiving of your desire is truth.

You must open your life up to what you are receiving. Open your heart, your mind, and your spirit. Open the door to the area of your life where you desire will enter. Whatever it is you want, know that it already exists for you and the Universe has an abundant supply to fulfil your every want and need.

An important part of the preparation process is revising your routine as if the best version of your life is the present version. Live your best day today. Enjoy the best that life has to offer today. Put on your best smile, your best attitude, and walk into greatness today.

> *Negativity deflects positivity.*

Be mindful of negativity. Your desire is on it's way. Giving your energy to negativity decreases the energy you are giving to the good coming into your life. Negativity deflects positivity. If you are complaining about what you do not have, then you are stopping yourself from receiving what you wish to have. If you are listening to the complaints and negativity of others, you are blocking the good coming into your life as well.

You have the power to create the world around you. Prepare for the best. Request the best. Believe the best is coming to you. Live the best version of your life in the present. There is no better time than the present to receive every good thing that exists for you.

Plant the Seed

"Die as I may, I want it said of me that I plucked a weed and planted a flower wherever I thought a flower might grow."

– Abraham Lincoln

As I've said before, people are like plants. Plants stem from a single seed. Over time, growth comes from the nourishment of that seed. Similarly, your positive and negative thoughts and behaviors stem from a seed that has been planted within you. You have the choice of which seeds you nourish and allow to grow.

A single seed holds all of the potential for growth and development for the thing that stems from it. With proper nourishment, the seed of an orange tree possesses the power to produce the orange tree along with its orange blossoms. Likewise, the seed of a single thought possesses the power to materialize the product of that thought in your life if you give energy to that thought. This is the process of cause and effect - the nourishment of the seed being the cause, the effect being the flower or the product of your thought.

> *The nourishment of the seed being the cause, the effect being the flower or the product of your thought.*

Once the orange tree has branched off and the flowers have bloomed, it produces its fruit. The oranges contain more seeds that can be planted and if nourished, will produce other trees, blossoms, and fruit. As your thoughts develop and you give attention to those thoughts, they will produce fruit that contain seeds that you can plant in other people.

We cannot control the thoughts and actions of others. With that being said, once you plant the seed of positivity into another person, you cannot nourish it for them. It is their responsibility. However, planting the seed of positivity can give them the ability to change their own life.

For some, that seed may linger for a while before the individual provides the nourishment required for growth. But if that person witnesses the abundance of good in your life, it may empower them to give more energy to their positive thoughts and allow the seed to sprout and bloom. Once those thoughts bloom, further nourishment will produce the fruit of positivity in their life and provide them with the seeds to plant in others as well.

You may be wondering, how do you do this? How do you plant the seed of positivity into another person? Listed below are three methods you can practice:

* Give "praise reports" - Share your good news with others and discuss how using positivity, gratitude, and love has impacted your life. This potentially plants the seed of positivity and may evoke their desire to nourish that seed and produce positive results.

* Give complements - Complement others often. It's always a confidence boost to receive complements on your appearance, your light, your skills, your abilities, and so on. Giving complements to others will also boost their confidence and plant the seeds of self-love and self-worth.

* Give reassurance - Acknowledge when you notice that others are making progress. When you commend others and reassure them that they are headed in a positive direction, it will motivate them to keep moving forward. Reassurance can also provide nourishment to the seed of positivity.

Plant seeds of positivity in the hearts of others. Plant seeds of gratitude, love, and abundance in their hearts; meanwhile, continue to nourish your own positive thoughts in order for them to continue to bloom. Will your life to be a garden of joy, beauty, and hope. With this intention, you are creating a positive environment for others to achieve greatness too.

Free Your Mind

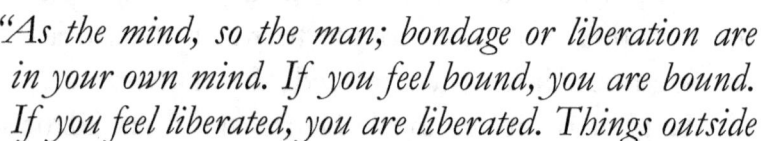

"As the mind, so the man; bondage or liberation are in your own mind. If you feel bound, you are bound. If you feel liberated, you are liberated. Things outside neither bind nor liberate you; only your attitude towards them does that."

- Swami Satchidananda

Freedom is normally associated with the ability to physically move without constraint or obstruction. Physical freedom allows you to go wherever you want to go whenever you want to go. This freedom is a privilege so often taken for granted and never truly enjoyed until you grasp its other half: freedom of your mind.

True freedom of mind comes with the ability to live above your circumstances and not be affected by negative situations or conditions that you come in contact with. Mental freedom brings awareness to the world around you and enables you to think clearly and proactively when you are faced with a challenge.

Do you remember how free your mind was at three years old? How about five years old? You were worry-free. You didn't dwell over the pain of the past or the pressure of the future. You only thought of the present moment. You didn't care about what others thought of you. You focused only on what made you happy, because what made you happy made you feel free.

As you transitioned into adolescence and adulthood, your outside circumstances began to seep into your mind. You started to believe in the beliefs and standards set by society regarding beauty, success, wealth, love, and perfection. You let those things become barriers to your thoughts and abilities, and you began to build walls around your mind in order to protect yourself from being hurt. Freedom of mind comes with breaking through those barriers. You must realize that the only person who can hurt you is YOU.

> *Even if you are physically free, mental confinement chains you to the past and dooms you to live in fear and resistance.*

It hurts you to live by the standards of society. It hurts you to believe the opinions of others. It hurts you to live in fear. By allowing such impacts from the outside, you are inevitably hurting yourself. Even if you are physically free, mental confinement chains you to the past and dooms you to live in fear and resistance. However, you have the power to set your own standards and beliefs and live in harmony and peace.

Bring back the mental state you maintained in your childhood. Let outside circumstances roll off your back. Don't give power to the opinions of others. Don't give power to negativity. Don't give power to the past or the future. Focus on what makes you happy in this moment. Go to your happy place in your mind and refuse to leave that state.

Think outside those barriers and limitations. Go beyond and be in a world in which YOU are a force, a champion, a hero. Love freely, laugh freely, believe freely, and embrace an abundance of freedom in every area of your life, so that you can live freely.

Believe in Magic

"Hatred paralyzes life; love releases it. Hatred confuses life; love harmonizes it. Hatred darkens life; love illuminates it."

- Martin Luther King, Jr.

Love is magic. The more love you give, the more love you receive in your life. Love is a powerful force that moves the world around you. It is the force that stirs the currents and heals the brokenness of our world.

Love exists in every equation and in every dynamic. Love wills the flowers to grow. Love warms the Earth. Love seeps through every smile and kind word. Love is the essence of all things. It ebbs and flows throughout the Universe.

Regardless of what name you use to refer to this force - the Supreme Mind, God, your Higher Self - Love is the law that governs the Universe. Love dwells in every tree, in every rock, and in every waterfall. Love moves the wind and falls with the rain. Love connects us to one another.

> *Love connects us to one another.*

That is the magic. Love is the answer. To believe in love is to believe in the solution to any problem or issue. Love heals, mends, recovers, revives, restores, and rebuilds. To feel love and believe in the power of love gives you the ability to receive and understand love.

You were made to give and receive love. The more love you pour into others, the more love is replenished in your life. Love more. Love in abundance. Love all things and all people. Love your circumstances. Let love encompass your life.

You must first give love inwardly before you can give it outwardly. Know that you are worthy of love. Give love to yourself. Focus on everything there is to love about you and allow that love to grow and spread through all of your being. Look in the mirror and say, "I love you, [your name.]" Do this multiple times every day and truly feel that love.

Wrap your thoughts, words, and actions in love. If you are thinking that you hate the conditions that you are in, you will receive more conditions that you will hate. If you hate that the is a lack of money in your life, you will continue to receive more debt and bills. If you hate that your marriage is falling apart, you will receive more brokenness in your relationships.

Be mindful of your complaints. That is not love. Instead of focusing your thoughts on what you don't love, refocus on what you do love. If you can't find things you love in your life, it may be a matter of simply opening your eyes.

Look around - the heavens and the Earth were created for you. The Universe moves for you. You are surrounded by the colors, sounds, and smells of nature and the perfect placement of all elements in this world. You are alive and able to enjoy all of this. Wake up and smell the roses. They bloom for you.

Love spreads like a wildfire. Feed that fire and let it destroy any resentment, anger, and any other ill feelings you hold in your heart. Let it blaze as high as you will it, so that it spreads light through the darkness that has taken a hold of your world. Love is the light. Darkness has no power here.

Love what you have in front of you right now. Love the people, things, and circumstances that make up your present moment. Love even your past and the lessons that you've learned throughout you life. When you are on the frequency of love, you will begin to see love infiltrate every area of your life.

Positive Perspective

"Optimism is the faith that leads to achievement."

- Helen Keller

We all know that in life bad things can happen; in fact, bad things *do* happen. The question isn't whether you are faced with negative circumstances, but how you perceive them and whether you find the good in them. If you don't like the way something looks, change the way you look at it.

Are you someone that sees the glass as half full or half empty? Do you see that the substance inside of the glass is running out, or do you see that there is simply room to add more substance? Regardless, the same amount is in each glass.

It's all about your perspective. If you see the glass as half full, then your perspective is positive and you're on the right track.

Your perspective of things creates the tone for your life. If you wake up in the morning with a positive perspective of how your day will unfold, then you will go through the day expecting good things to happen. Even if bad instances occur, you will be more likely to notice the good in those instances. However, if you wake up with a negative perspective of your day and you maintain that throughout the morning, guess what? You won't expect good and you won't be open to receiving good things. The plus side is that you can change your perspective easily.

When you find yourself thinking that everything is going wrong and things can't get any worse than they are now, refocus those thoughts. Don't give them any power. If things can't get any wore, then that means things can only get better, right? Therefore, you should focus on better. Take time to recollect yourself and know that you're on the verge of a breakthrough. Feel the good coming from the Universe and into your life, taking over your day, and wrapping you in positivity.

See endless possibilities of the good circumstances that are likely to come into your life. See everything that you've managed to accomplish today. See all of the love that is surrounding you. See the darkness fading and the light coming into your life. When rain clouds roll in and darken your sky, it is important for you to remember that every dark cloud has a silver lining.

If rain clouds are in the sky blocking the light from the sun, that doesn't mean the sun has stopped shining. The sun never ceases to shine. Through hurricanes, tornadoes, thunderstorms, and blizzards the sun continues to radiate its brilliant light. Whether it's day or night, whether you can see it or not, the sun glistens boldly. Not even darkness could stop it from fulfilling its purpose. Darkness cannot prevent you from shining either.

Blessings shimmer in those temporary moments of darkness. The key word is temporary. The bad isn't perpetual. You will overcome it. You will come out of it stronger, braver, and more powerful. Through the bad, you may even find better circumstances, better people, and better qualities within yourself.

> *Blessings shimmer in those temporary moments of darkness.*

If you are seeing your life as a half empty glass, then you should instead see all of the ways that you can fill that glass up. If you notice nothing but dark clouds in your sky, then look beyond those clouds and see all of the luminous forms of light that are lighting up your world. Change your perspective, make it positive, and you will see your life in a way you have never seen before.

Dare to Dream

"All our dreams can come true, if we have the courage to pursue them."

- Walt Disney

What wish is your heart making? What is your dream? Do you dream to have a family? Do you dream to be a doctor or a fashion designer? Do you dream to publish a novel or play the lead role in an action film? Do you dream to travel the world or visit outer-space? Whatever you can dream, you can achieve.

Your purpose is to enjoy life and live in harmony within your own dream. You were created to reap the benefits that life has to offer you. You don't have to ask permission to enjoy it.

Be brave and unapologetic. All you must do is envision your dream and reach for it.

When you were a child you were fearless. Pain was temporary and suffering was brief. Thoughts of failure, rejection, and heartache did not stop you from following your dream. Each day was a new day of exciting adventures. You built forts out of pillows and blankets and set up camp in the enchanted forest. You had a twig that was really a magic wand. You lived in the dream that you created. No one could convince you that it wasn't real or that it wasn't yours.

Eventually, you decided you wanted to be a doctor when you got older. Day after day, you practiced your doctoring skills. You scheduled appointments for your stuffed animals and checked their pulse with your plastic stethoscope. You knew that you'd be a great doctor and possibly even cure every disease on the entire planet. No one could detour you from your dream.

One disease you weren't prepared for then was the "You Can't" Disease. In your childhood, you had such hope in your dream that you wanted to share the dream with others. You told your parents, your teachers, and your peers about your dream. You shared with others that you would be the best doctor in the country and cure all the disease in the nation, maybe even the whole world. And what did they tell you? "You Can't."

You were in such disbelief. But more and more people told you "You Can't," and you started to believe it. The disease began to spread through your being and your dream began to fade. Whatever your dream is, if you choose to allow the "You Can't" Disease to spread, you will believe that your dream is not yours, that you cannot and will not achieve it.

It is not the role of another person to tell you what to dream, how to dream, or when to dream. No one can see your dream. No one can stop you from seeing your dream either, unless of course you allow them to block your view or blur your focus. Do not allow the "You Can't" Disease to spread within you.

Dare to dream. Dream big and believe in your dream. Dare to defy the odds. Dare to create a dream that is beautiful and magical and unbelievable. Have child-like faith and do not let anyone detour you from your dream. The magic wand is in your hand. You can do anything you set your mind to. Remember that this is your dream - if you don't love it, you have the power to create a new dream. The choice is yours.

> *Have child-like faith and do not let anyone detour you from your dream.*

Unveil the Unseen

"Dream lofty dreams, and as you dream, so you shall become. Your vision is the promise of what you shall one day be your ideal is the prophecy of what you shall at last reveal."

- James Allen

From the very beginning, the Universe was orchestrated to the point of perfection. There is nothing to add, nor is there anything to be taken away. All that was, is, and ever will be came into existence at once. As humans, we have attained more knowledge and awareness of those creations. We are beginning to realize the ability we have to transform the world around us. That ability lies within you.

For some, the phrase "seeing is believing" is their truth. But as you will learn throughout the pages of this book, seeing comes secondary to believing. In order to see your dream become reality, you must believe that it already exists. If you can imagine it and believe it, then you will see it in your life.

Imagine that the very thing you desire to have is inside of a cardboard box. The box is sealed shut and you cannot see the contents inside. You walk past this box day after day completely unaware. Meanwhile, you believe that what you want does exist. You believe you are worthy and you believe it is yours.

One day, you finally bring your attention to this box and have a strong urge to open it. You are hesitant at first, but you feel the urge growing and assuring you the box belongs to you. You get closer and you are excited to realize that the box is addressed to you, so you open it. What does the box contain?

The very thing you wanted was close to you all along. You may not have realized it at first, but your belief in it brought it into your point of focus. You took a step forward in faith and lifted the lid to unveil the unseen.

> *There are no limitations to what you can have, achieve, or be.*

This is the case for all of your desires. There are no limitations to what you can have, achieve, or be. Size does not matter to the Universe. If you label something as too big or too small, that label only becomes an excuse that hinders you from receiving the good you deserve. The good that exists for you. The good that sits in the box addressed to you. It is up to you to believe.

Whatever you wish to bring into your world, you must hold the image of it in your mind. Perceive your present life as if you have your desire now and remember to feel gratitude for it. Believing gives you the ability to see what's yours. It doesn't matter if others believe in it or not, because it is for you and only you. There is no better day than today to unveil the unseen in your life and transform your world.

Faith, No Fear

"As we are liberated from our own fear, our presence automatically liberates others."

- Marianne Williamson

In the presence of faith, fear has no place. Likewise, in the presence of fear, faith does not exist. The two cannot exist together. Faith is truth; fear is an illusion. Fear stops you from pursuing your dreams. Fear stops you from growth and healing. Fear stops you from giving and receiving love and trust, while faith allows you to do so.

Fear grabs a hold of your heart and causes you to build walls up that block things from coming into your life. You may think you are only blocking out the bad to protect yourself from pain. In reality, those walls also block the good. Those walls prevent movement and cause you to become stagnant. You may eventually feel stuck and hopeless.

Brick by brick, you have built this wall. It is large and strong. There are vines growing up the sides. There are birds of many colors that perch at the top of the wall and ant hills that have formed at the base. Your wall blocks out bad weather to keep you dry, but it's also blocking out the sunlight and warmth. You never know if it's day or night - you just know that time is passing you by.

These bricks have names: Reluctance, Resistance, and Hesitance. Each of the bricks are cemented in fear. Fear to move forward. Fear of the unknown. Fear of failure. Fear of unworthiness. Fear of vulnerability. Reluctance sets in when you are unwilling to take action. Resistance sets in when you struggle against action. Hesitance sets in when you delay action due to doubt.

Thoughts of fear produce more fear as a result, you build more reluctance, resistance, and hesitance. Brick by brick you are closing out the beauty of the world and the opportunities that exist for you. The good news is that brick by brick you can tear that wall down and let the light back into your life. Don't just let time pass by. You can open your life up to new opportunities, new people, and new experiences. How? By faith.

To have faith is to trust and believe in the power of the Universe. It is to believe that no matter the circumstances, things will work out for good and you will come out of all experiences stronger than before. It is to know without a shadow of doubt that the intention for your life is great and that there is an abundance of love and joy in the Universe for you.

Even if you aren't taking a leap of faith just yet, take the first step in faith. Knock out the first brick. Overcome reluctance with the inclination to act in faith. Overcome resistance with the determination to advance in faith. Overcome hesitance with the readiness to discredit your doubts and be your own superhero.

> *Even if you aren't taking a leap of faith just yet, take the first step in faith.*

Let faith lead you to take risks that will improve your life. Be brave. Be bold. Stay true to yourself and believe in your ability to be victorious. Allow the wall you've built to come down brick by brick. Let the light in and let it direct you. Trust that you are headed in the right direction and have no fear of defeat or default. Your faith is your compass - it will never lead you astray.

Breathe

"Trying to meditate with a head full of desires is like a plane trying to take off with too much cargo. Planes must offload the cargo to take flight. Just as humans must offload their desires to be able to meditate."

- Swami A. Parthasarthy

When we are infants and toddlers there are many things we are taught to do - to walk, to talk, to hold a bottle, a spoon, a pencil. One thing we are not taught is how to breathe. It's natural from birth. Breathing keeps you alive. You can live without walking or talking, but you cannot live without breathing.

Although breathing isn't normally something we are taught to do in our youth, it should be. The importance and impact of breathing should be taught. The privilege and need of thankfulness for breathing should be taught. Specifically, the art of mindful breathing should be taught.

You have read about many different variations of the give and receive process so far. This process exists with your breathing as well. The trees are giving you the oxygen you need to breathe and in turn the trees are receiving the carbon dioxide they need to grow from you. It's a never ending cycle.

As you inhale and exhale you are also circulating energy. You are breathing in energy and breathing out energy. When you are thinking and feeling good, you are circulating positive energy with your breathing. Similarly, when you are thinking and feeling bad, you are circulating negative energy. If you are feeling bad, you can consciously decide to exhale all of the negative energy and inhale the good.

Breathing not only impacts your physical body, it also impacts your mental health. When you are feeling emotions such as anxiety, anger, or anxiousness, mindful breathing exercises can quiet your mind and calm your negative thoughts. Mindful breathing takes your thoughts away from your circumstances and focuses your mind on your breathing in the present moment. This allows you to balance and stabilize your mind and creates a healthier state for reflection and resolution.

Mindfulness meditation is one practice that may help you to strengthen your mind into being more aware of your breathing. It may help you to practice alone and in a quiet place, but overtime you will be able to breathe mindfully at any time and in any environment.

Yoga is also a practice that can improve your mindfulness of breathing. Through the transition between poses and during the holding of poses you will become more aware of how your breathing impacts your balance as well as your concentration.

Every breath you take is a gift - a privilege. Each breath is a reason to be thankful. Feeling gratitude for breathing is a way to change the energy you are circulating. When you are feeling bad, take a moment to pause and take a few deep breaths. Be thankful for those breaths. Be thankful for the trees and the oxygen and the other elements that are keeping you alive. Be thankful for your lungs that are working tirelessly to circulate the oxygen.

> *Feeling gratitude for breathing is a way to change the energy you are circulating.*

The gratitude you feel for breathing will enhance your experiences. That gratitude will increase your awareness of the gift you've been given and allow you to reach your full potential to live in abundance. Do not take a single breath for granted, because without it you would not be alive. Without it you would not experience love or joy or peace. With it, you will achieve greatness.

Be a Lighthouse

"Lighthouses don't go running all over an island looking for boats to save, they just stand there shining."

— Anne LaMotte

A lighthouse is a structure with a magnificently bright light that shines to guide sailors to shore. A light so bright that it pierces through severe weather, dense fog, and unyielding darkness in order to guide sailors to safety. A light that gives them reassurance that they are nearing the shore and should continue to tread forward with hope and determination.

There are many moments in life when the weather is severe and we lose our way. Darkness comes in many different forms: divorce, unemployment, incarceration, sickness, the loss of a loved one, addiction, etc. Negative circumstances rain down on you and may cause you to lose focus. These circumstances seep in and weigh you down causing you to feel heavy, vulnerable, and - worst of all - alone. However, you are not alone. There are others who are suffering and searching for the shoreline as well.

Do you recall a moment in your life when you needed encouragement? Reassurance? Guidance? When you felt like you were fighting against impossible odds and there was no way out? In that very moment, you may have heard someone you esteem on television saying the very thing you needed to hear. Maybe you were listening to the radio and heard something inspiring and felt that the words were directed towards you. Maybe someone in your life discussed their success story with you and you realized that they are where you aspire to be. When someone crosses your path that is achieving what you wish to achieve, know that they are put there to show you that not only is it possible for you, but also that you are nearing the shore of your dream.

There are moments when the very thing that you need is the very thing you become. As you receive inspiration and motivation from another individual, someone may be receiving those things from you as well. When you move towards the thing that guides you to hope, others begin to draw near you. The thing you need in your life is the thing you ARE in the lives of others.

The most important thing to realize in these moments is that there is a light within you. We all posses a light, a natural aura. That light shines when you hold out your hand to help someone up who has fallen down. It shines when you smile at a stranger. It shines through your random acts of kindness and kind words. As you give love outwardly, the love within you increases and your light shines brighter.

When you find the light within you and allow it to illuminate your world, darkness will no longer prevail. Others will become curious of the source of your light and discover that they hold the same power within. Eventually, they become a lighthouse for another and the cycle of hope will continue on indefinitely.

Remember that every person you meet is experiencing their own form of darkness and pushing through their own storm. There may be times when you will come across an individual who may not openly discuss their circumstances with you, or anyone for that matter. You must remember that seeing you push through with purpose and lead by example may encourage them to do the same - just as the example of others has inspired you. Shining your light may reveal to them that they are closer to the shore than they may have realized. Your light has that kind of power.

> *It's important that you shine your light even when you think no one is looking.*

It's important that you shine your light even when you think no one is looking. I assure you, someone is always looking. Whether you realize it or not, you are someone's lighthouse. Someone will always be in need of your guidance and your encouragement. Let that instill within you a greater sense of purpose.

You will find that it cost nothing to offer words of encouragement and empowerment to those whose lights have been dimmed, although the reward is more than money can afford. There are 36,400 seconds in each day of your life, and it only takes a few seconds to make a difference in someone's life. Only a few seconds to give someone hope and inspire them to believe that they too can outshine the darkness. How many seconds are you willing to spare?

Be the leader you wish to follow. Hold out the hand you wish to grab. Speak the words you wish to hear. Give the love you wish to receive. And above all, make it your intention to stand there and shine your light for those who are in the midst of a storm and are looking to you to guide them to shore.

SPREAD THE JEWELS

"It's greedier to withhold knowledge than it is to withhold riches. The lessons learned in life are permanent jewels - gifts from the Universe that can never be taken away. These gifts are meant to be shared with others. It's not your concern to worry about if they use them or not or how they'll use them. Spread the wealth!"

– Brandon Francois

A jewel is a precious stone of great value to the one who treasures it. Typically, the story of how a person gains possession of the jewel is what makes the stone rather priceless. But you will find that your jewels will become more valuable as you pay them forward.

Experience is undeniably the most effective teacher that you will encounter in this life. Through all of the mistakes, setbacks, downfalls, obstacles, hardships, and tribulations that you face in life, there is always a lesson to be learned. These moments in life sharpen your mind. These moments are character building exercises. Each time you fall, you will get back up even wiser than before. In these pivotal moments, you will learn what it means to begin again.

Through the pain that you endure, you learn the extent of your resilience, tolerance, and strength. However, you don't necessarily have to experience pain to gain. We hear it all the time, right? "No pain, no gain." This isn't always the case. In the beautiful moments of life, you also learn things about yourself and the world around you. Just as pain produces jewels, so does beauty.

Through acts of appreciation, kindness, understanding, compassion, love, commitment, etc., you uncover the jewels that have always been stored in your heart. Similarly, you will find precious jewels that exist in your mind through good memories. Many of us recall bad experiences and bad memories leading us to think that our life was "all bad." Life isn't all bad though, is it?

For example, think back to a moment of completion in your life - when you graduated kindergarten, high school, possibly college. Maybe you've obtained your GED/HiSet. Maybe you've completed a certification, or a few. Each of these completions reflects your potential, your ability to achieve, and your determination. When you think back on things you've learned and accomplished, it can fuel you to push further and accomplish another, then another, then another goal.

Another example of a good memory can be an instance when you taught someone. Teaching others is a method of spreading the jewels that can generate good memories. Teaching others also gives you you a sense of accomplishment. Maybe you taught your child how to ride a bike. Maybe you facilitated a class or tutored someone who needed one-on-one. Maybe you taught someone to change a tire. In these moments, you passed on knowledge to another person that was needed in order for them to continue to progress.

When others are learning from you, you are nourishing them and helping them to succeed. Remember that just as the student learns from the teacher, so does the teacher learn from the student - both are spreading the jewels. These interactions with others strengthen your communication skills, develop your trust in others, and allow you to build relationships.

When you find yourself thinking that life is all bad, look for the good, remember the good, and focus on the good that exists in your life. It's important to be aware of the blessings and better opportunities that can arise from negative circumstances. That awareness makes you more receptive to learning. As you know, learning is essential to growth and development. Furthermore, with the gaining of knowledge comes the responsibility to teach others.

You have the responsibility to pass the knowledge on to your children, your family, your friends, people you know, as well as people you may not know. Even if they do not apply the lessons right then, it's important that you share. That jewel may become vital to them at a later point in their life. Its value may appreciate over time.

Your story is what makes you unique. You, yourself, are a jewel - a diamond in the rough. You shimmer and sparkle in the sunlight. You have made your way through the darkness. Through the bright and the dark moments in your life, there were many things you had to learn in order to get where you are now. As you share your story with others, you are giving them a different perspective in which they can view their life. You are supplying them with tools to work through their own rubble and build a stronger foundation.

> *As you share your story with others, you are giving them a different perspective in which they can view their life.*

    You are improving the world by spreading the jewels. Sharing knowledge is an act of love. And as you know, love is the most powerful force in the Universe. You can spread the jewels by sharing your experiences, by leading by example, or by encouraging others. You can be creative with it. Regardless of how you choose to spread the jewels, let it always be with love. In doing this, you are increasing the good in the world. You are making a difference.

The Closing: Uncovering the Meaning of H.O.P.E.

"By this means you will acquire the glory of the whole world."

-The Emerald Tablet

Hope is an essence, just as it is an action. Hope is what things are made of. It is an energy, a living and breathing force. Hope instills your being and pulls you into the realm of your truest desires. Hope ignites the fuse that you didn't realize existed. It moves you to follow your wildest dreams. Hope evokes courage and passion. It wills you to believe.

If you have hope, you have something. There are many moments in life where we feel it is easier to give up. To sit down and let life take its course. We are told that we have no say so in what happens to us. Over time, we believe that as truth. However, it is the complete opposite.

You have say so in how you think, how you feel, how you act and react. You have say so in what you choose to believe. All of the things that come into your life are things that you have willed into existence. They are things you have believed in. That is the power you have within you, the power to believe.

That is where hope comes in. It is our hope that keeps our beliefs intact. We hope for better, we believe that better exists, and we will it into existence in our life. That is the formula. That is truth. And the most essential action in keeping your hope alive is your ability to H.O.P.E. - And here, we uncover the meaning.

H.O.P.E. is to Hold On to Positive Energy. It is to release all negativity in your life and focus on the good. It is to feel gratitude and love for all things and all people. It is to smile and laugh and feel joy. You must feed your hope the way you feed a campfire - breathe life into it. If your flame starts to burn out, remember all of the ways there are to Hold On to Positive Energy.

As you strengthen your ability to H.O.P.E., you will see your life evolve in the most astounding ways. Your hope is within you, it can never be taken from you. You have always possessed this amazing power - it's time to utilize it. Always remember that you are responsible for your own happiness. Prepare for the best and know that YOU deserve the best. You are a light. Shine bright and always believe in yourself.

H.O.P.E.

H.O.P.E. Challenges

I've designed these challenges for you to put the H.O.P.E. methods to practice and get the most out of this book. These challenges are not mandatory and there is no specific order or time period for you to complete them however, upon completing each challenge, you will have increased your awareness of the positivity in your life and strengthen your ability to Hold On to Positive Energy. For the best results, I recommend keeping a H.O.P.E. journal so that you can record your reflections and gratitude there.

Follow the Stars Challenge

1. Think of whether you have already discovered your symbol of hope. If you have not, this is your moment. Decide what your symbol of hope is - a butterfly? a number? a color? a flower? a certain word? What resonates with you most?

2. Know that your symbol of hope will guide you throughout your life and lead you in the direction towards the best version of your life. If you are walking down the wrong path, commit to changing your direction for the better.

Reflect: Consider the impact that having hope has in your life. Are you looking for reassurance that you are on the right path now? Do you believe that the best version of your life exists for you? Remember that you are worthy of a good life, even if you have made mistakes in the past. How does that make you feel?

Follow the Stars and you will be guided to H.O.P.E.

Encourage Yourself Challenge

1. Just like in the Believe in Magic chapter, you will look in the mirror today and speak love over yourself. As you stare at your own reflection, recite these words out loud and clearly: I am powerful. I will overcome. I am great. I will reach my full potential. I can do anything. I will *succeed*.

2. Repeat this practice throughout the day each time you pass by a mirror. Feel and believe that these words are your truth and continue to encourage yourself through moments of uncertainty.

Reflect: Consider how it felt to speak words of encouragement over yourself. Do you feel empowered? Do you feel that you can do anything? How could reciting these words daily motivate you to persist and strive to accomplish your goals? Put your answer to the test and practice this daily. Turn possibilities into probabilities.

Encourage Yourself and reach your full potential to H.O.P.E.

KNOW YOUR WORTH CHALLENGE

1. Sit in a quiet place and think of three different occasions when you believed in your self-worth. Was there a time when you forgave yourself? A time when you fell and got back up to try again? A time when you were thankful for your strengths, talents, and skills? A time when you refused to settle for less?

2. Thank yourself for those occasions and your belief in your worth.

Reflect: Consider the outcome of those occasions and think about how you felt. How can knowing your worth impact your life moving forward? Are you in a situation now in which you are questioning your worth? How will you resolve that situation?

Know Your Worth - that knowledge is the key to H.O.P.E.

Let Go and Hold On Challenge

1. Make a conscious decision to let go of three negative weights in your life today. These weights can include a material, a person, a habit, a circumstance or condition in your life.

2. Once you've decided on the weights, consider three positive replacements you will hold on to instead. Is there opportunities you'd like to take part in? Are you wanting to get to know someone new?

Reflect: Think about the difference in your spirit now that you have replaced three negatives with three positives in your life. Do you feel lighter? Do you have more energy? How will applying this to your daily or weekly routine alter your life? How does that make you feel?

Let Go and H.O.P.E.

Gratitude Brings Good Challenge

1. Write a list of all of the good in your life right now - good news, good experiences, good opportunities, good relationships, etc. - count all of your blessings. For each blessing you list, feel gratitude and think of at least one way that this blessing positively impacts your life.

2. Throughout the day, review your list and continue to give thanks for the good in your life. Give thanks for the good news that others share with you today as well. Know that you are on a good news frequency and feel gratitude for that confirmation.

Reflect: Consider how feeling gratitude for the blessings in your life made you feel today. Also consider how it felt to be thankful for the good news to others. What positive ways can practicing gratitude daily impact your present conditions?

Gratitude Brings Good into your life and strengthens your ability to H.O.P.E.

Prepare to Receive Challenge

1. Think about what it is that you want most at this present moment? Prepare to receive it now.

2. Believe that this desire has arrived and you are receiving it today. Live today as if you have your desire. Perhaps you wish to get a new job? Believe that you have the job of your dreams and revise your day according to receiving that job. Continue to practice this daily.

Reflect: Consider the impact that living the best version of your life in the present will have on your present and your future. What is the harm in negativity? How can positivity impact your life? Why would you wait to live the best day of your life tomorrow? How will it feel for you to live your best day today and every day that follows?

Prepare to Receive through your power to H.O.P.E.

Plant the Seed Challenge

1. Put the three methods of planting the seed of positivity into practice today. Find three people who you will share good news with, give a complement, and offer reassurance that they are headed in a positive direction. You can use one method per person, or all three methods for each person.

2. Take notes of how you felt before, during, and after you planted the seed - was there a shift in your energy? Did the other person's energy shift during the conversation?

Reflect: At the end of the day, think back to each exchange and consider how planting the seed of positivity in others influenced your own growth and development. Was there an increase in positivity in your own thoughts and feelings? How can this practice impact the world around you?

Plant the Seed of positivity in others and instill within them the desire to H.O.P.E.

Free Your Mind Challenge

1. Find a quiet place at one point in your day, and think about places that you've been or moments in your life when you felt happy and free.

2. Once you've thought through these moments in your life, choose one place or moment and visualize yourself there for five minutes. Feel the happiness and freedom of that memory in the present moment.

Reflect: Consider how revisiting happy moments may increase your ability to free your mind when negative circumstances may be affecting you. How can seeing yourself happy and at peace in this moment redirect your focus? How can practicing this everyday strengthen your mind and impact your own mental freedom?

Free Your Mind - live in your happy place and H.O.P.E.

BELIEVE IN MAGIC CHALLENGE

1. Find time today to sit with a pen and paper and write down everything you love. Think through all areas of your life: your career, your finances, your health, your relationships, and your personal desires. Think about things you love in nature, places you'd love to go, and things you'd love to do.

2. After you write your list, take time to feel love for all of the things you've written down. Let that love flow through your life.

Reflect: Consider all of the things worth loving in your life. How did you feel after you wrote it all out? Were you surprised? Is there more that you could add to the list? If you did this challenge every month, how would it impact the love you feel in your life?

Believe in Magic and let it flow through your life as you H.O.P.E.

POSITIVE PERSPECTIVE CHALLENGE

1. Practice using your positive perspective today. Think about whether you are in a situation that you are currently perceiving as negative. It could be something that recently happened or something that is happening now.

2. Shift your perspective to positivity and determine the good in that situation. Look at it from different angles and think of all of the ways it could work out in your favor and have a positive outcome.

Reflect: Consider how shifting into a positive perspective can impact your life. How did seeing this situation as beneficial to you change the way you felt towards the situation? In the future, be mindful when you shift back into a negative perspective and put this challenge into practice again.

Practice a Positive Perspective and discover all of the ways there are to H.O.P.E.

Dare to Dream Challenge

1. Today, you will think back to your childhood dream. What did you dream to become? To do? Think back to times when you shared your dream with others and you were discouraged, then you allowed the "You Can't" Disease to spread.

2. Create a new dream today. Commit to your dream and decide that you will not let anyone detour you, that you can do anything, and you will achieve your dream. Take a moment to write down your dream and all of the ways you will enjoy achieving and living that dream.

Reflect: Consider how discouraging someone from their dream impacts their growth. What ways can you encourage others to follow their dreams? What ways can you ensure that you continue to believe in your own dreams?

Dare to Dream - create a dream that's magical as you H.O.P.E.

Unveil the Unseen Challenge

1. Today, focus on one thing you desire to have Find a quiet place to sit and write a list of every way that desire will change your life: how will it impact your routine, your well-being, your feelings, etc.

2. Once you've made your list, consider the negative thoughts you have towards not having your desire - Do you think you are unworthy or your desire is insignificant? Find positive thoughts to counteract these excuses.

Reflect: Consider whether there is a box in your life that you are passing by without notice. Do you believe your desire is yours? How can countering negative beliefs daily bring awareness to the good that already exists in your life?

Unveil the Unseen and expand your capacity to H.O.P.E.

Faith, No Fear Challenge

1. Determine the action(s) you need to take that you are showing reluctance, resistance, and/or hesitance towards. What is the action(s)? What's stopping you from acting? What are your fears?

2. Acknowledge that having faith in the positive outcome of your action will increase your inclination, determination, and readiness to act and succeed. Do not give power to fear. Decide today that you will take action and take the first step in faith.

Reflect: Consider how it felt to have faith and take the first step towards your goal or dream. How did it feel to make that progress? What power does faith have over your fears? How can knocking down that wall impact your ability to move forward and grow?

Faith, No Fear - let this be your motto that inspires you to H.O.P.E.

Breathe Challenge

1. Find a quiet place to sit or lie down comfortably. Close your eyes and focus on your natural breathing. As you inhale, notice the rise of your chest and your stomach. As you exhale, notice the fall.

2. As your thoughts drift away, refocus on your breathing. Notice the weight of your body and the sensations that you are feeling. Notice the pause between your breaths. After about five minutes, bring awareness back to the present and feel gratitude for your mindful breathing.

Reflect: Consider how mindful breathing impacts your mental state and your physical condition. How did you feel after this challenge? How can gratitude for your breathing impact your life on a daily basis? How can doing this challenge daily impact the energy you are circulating?

Breathe and feel gratitude for that gift in order for you to H.O.P.E.

BE A LIGHTHOUSE CHALLENGE

1. Give a genuine smile to each person that passes you throughout the day today.

2. Make a mental note of whether you recognize a shift in their energy, posture, and/or expression. Did they hold their head up higher afterwards? Walk more swiftly? Walk with a stronger sense of confidence?

Reflect: At the end of the day, think back on how others responded to your smile today. How did those responses make you feel? How might your life be impacted if you practiced this challenge daily? How might it impact the lives of others who cross paths with you?

Be a Lighthouse and shine a light on the way to H.O.P.E.

SPREAD THE JEWELS CHALLENGE

1. Find a quiet moment during your day to identify the lessons you've learned from the greatest hardships you've experienced, as well as the best memories you cherish. In what ways did you grow? Were you made stronger? How did you make it through?

2. Set up a time with someone important to you, so that you can share those jewels with them. Help them to identify the jewels they possess as well. Possibly come up with ways you can Spread the Jewels together.

Reflect: Consider the importance of spreading the jewels. How can this help and enlighten others? How does sharing this knowledge make you feel? What ways can you ensure that you continue to practice this?

Spread the Jewels and enlighten others of what it means to H.O.P.E.

Afterword

During the process of writing this book, I was incarcerated at the Louisiana Correctional Institute for Women serving a 35 year sentence. By the time I started outlining the chapters of H.O.P.E., I had already filed a petition for Post-Conviction Relief. I felt confident that my freedom was close, and I wanted to work consistently in order to finish the book before my release.

Writing H.O.P.E. was an amazing experience. All of the methods to Hold On to Positive Energy that I covered in the book are methods that I have discovered throughout my life, especially throughout my incarceration, so actually writing it all down and seeing it all fall together in one place was really awe inspiring. The process motivated me to continue to live by those methods and inspire others to do so as well.

As I said in the foreword, I was 17 years old when I was arrested and when I began to write H.O.P.E. I had been incarcerated for 6 years. Within those 6 years, I learned what rehabilitation truly means. It isn't a process that depends on the facility or the environment you are in - although, a positive environment is more conducive to growth - it has to do with your desire to reform and renew your mind and spirit as well as your determination to do so. Rehabilitation is an internal process. A process you have to commit to and be consistent in following through with.

Prison has a way of breaking you apart and leaving you to build from the ground up. However, life isn't about whether you fall apart, but what new masterpiece you create with the pieces. When there are more pieces to work with possibilities are endless. And once you are able to put those pieces together, others will be amazed to see the YOU that you've become.

No matter where you are - whether you are reading this in a prison cell, on your lunch break at your office, or sitting back on your Lazy Boy recliner at home - you can create a better life, a better world, and it starts within. In the words of the great Michael Jackson, "If you want to make the world a better place, take a look at yourself and make a change." That's your cue!

Thank you, reader, for joining me on this journey. I hope that *H.O.P.E.* resonates with you and plants a seed within you that flourishes and prospers. I also hope that you pass on what you've discovered to others and continue to spread the jewels. Strive to make a difference. Don't settle for just making a ripple in the pond, use your power to create waves in the ocean.

Acknowledgments

This journey has been a marvelous one. The gratitude that I feel for each individual in my life cannot be truly expressed through words.

There are so many people to thank for so many reasons in regard to the completion of this book; however, in order to keep it short, I will say this:

If you are reading this and we have not yet crossed paths, then know that I am grateful for your willingness to learn from me. The power lies within the knowledge we share, not the knowledge we hold.

To those who have loved me fearlessly, those who have believed in my vision, and those who have encouraged me to add a little glitter where necessary: my deepest gratitude to each of you. And to my lighthouses – you know who you are – thank you for seeing me to shore.

A much deserved and special thanks to Mr. Frank, Miss Quincy, and the phenomenal team at Cadmus Publishing for helping me bring my vision into fruition. Thank you for being just as dedicated to my dream as I am. Most importantly, thank you for what you do for incarcerated authors and keeping their hopes alive.

ABOUT THE AUTHOR

Brittany Monk, from South Louisiana, is 25 years old. Although incarcerated, she is pursuing a Bachelor's of Arts in Social Sciences at Tulane University. Her children's book, *Practice Makes Permanent*, was written in hopes of empowering our youth. In releasing her second book, *H.O.P.E.*, she hopes to encourage personal growth and self-love in each of her readers.

www.ingramcontent.com/pod-product-compliance
Lightning Source LLC
Chambersburg PA
CBHW071904070526
44583CB00016B/1835